Frank Lloyd Wright's
IMPERIAL

HOTEL

by CARY JAMES

DOVER PUBLICATIONS, INC.
New York

Quotations from *An Autobiography* and *Frank Lloyd Wright on Architecture* by Frank Lloyd Wright, reprinted by permission of Duell, Sloan & Pearce, Inc.

Published in Canada by General Publishing Company, Ltd.,
30 Lesmill Road, Don Mills, Toronto, Ontario.

This Dover edition, first published in 1988, is an unabridged, slightly altered republication of the work originally published by the Charles E. Tuttle Company, Rutland, Vermont, and Tokyo, Japan, in 1968, under the title *The Imperial Hotel: Frank Lloyd Wright and the Architecture of Unity*. The plans of the hotel, foldouts in the original edition, are here reproduced as double-page spreads. The present edition is published by special arrangement with the Charles E. Tuttle Company, Inc., Suido 1-chome, 2–6, Bunkyo-ku, Tokyo.

Manufactured in the United States of America
Dover Publications, Inc.
31 East 2nd Street
Mineola, N.Y. 11501

Library of Congress Cataloging-in-Publication Data

James, Cary, 1935–
[Imperial Hotel]
Frank Lloyd Wright's Imperial Hotel / by Cary James.
p.   cm.
Reprint. Originally published: The Imperial Hotel.
Rutland, Vt. : C.E. Tuttle Co., c1968.
Bibliography: p.
ISBN 0-486-25683-9 (pbk.)
1. Wright, Frank Lloyd, 1867–1959—Criticism and interpretation.
2. Teikoku Hoteru.   3. Architecture, American—Japan—Tokyo.
4. Architecture, Modern—20th century—Japan—Tokyo.   I. Title.
NA737.W7J33   1988
728′.5′0924—dc19   88-490
CIP

❖ TABLE OF CONTENTS ❖

❖ PREFACE ❖

Frank Lloyd Wright's Imperial Hotel building first began as a design on his boards in 1915. Construction was started in 1917 and the hotel opened in 1922. In 1923 it survived almost intact a major earthquake which ruined much of Tokyo, a feat that was to become its most famous statistic. As a hotel, the building functioned for 45 years; on November 15, 1967 the doors were closed and despite a last minute effort to save it, demolition began shortly thereafter.

This blunt chronology conceals both the glory of the building's existence and the tragedy of its end. Both of these—the reality of the hotel as art and the near-inevitability of its demise—are aspects of a single whole. The last twenty years saw the building crumble at an accelerating pace. The reasons for this are numerous. The face of the hotel was disfigured by the collapse of the soft stone in the industrial atmosphere of modern Tokyo. Structural sag and cracking were produced when a subway was constructed beneath one of the bedroom wings. A management no longer sensitive to the building added airconditioning and extra electrical equipment, and remodeled parts of the building, all in a heavy-handed manner. With travelers accustomed to the bright, wide spaces of newer hotels, the actual design became unpopular. The intense pressures of land values demanded a far more intensive use of the site. But all these facts are symptoms of a more essential problem, and this deeper reason is one of the concerns of this book.

Yet to dwell on the tragedy of the Imperial's final days is to obscure the real nature of the building. It is the vigor and vitality of its architect which illuminated the whole structure. The photographs do not emphasize the ruins though they are there; rather they look at those parts of the building which at the time—1965—were in moderate repair. Both pictures and text were completed before the end of the building had been absolutely confirmed. Both thus refer to it as if it continued to exist. Because I see Wright's idea of unity as an important, even necessary, addition to the traditions of the West, I have no desire to treat either the ideas or the building as antique history.

This book will appear after the end of the building; whatever value it might have offered in the attempt to save the structure will have passed, and it can be now only an incomplete, personal view of Wright's hotel. Yet perhaps the tragic end of this building can serve as stimulant in the future. Almost everywhere, buildings of worth are being threatened by the changing pressures of the times. Often there seems to be no way to save them, no way to reintegrate them into the stream of life. If this book can make us aware of what we have here destroyed, it may rededicate our efforts toward maintaining those works of art which still exist.

Yet the drive for preservation is itself not enough. The art of architecture requires the vigorous presence of life; to restore the form without the spirit of life is to embalm rather than to rejuvenate. We must continue our heritage not as artifact but as the image and shape of ongoing life. The thrust and the vigor which brings a building into being must remain with it, or it will stand as an empty corpse. "What is architecture anyway? . . . I know that architecture is life; or at least it is life itself taking *form*. . . . It can never be something which consists of the buildings which have been built by man on earth . . . mostly now a rubbish heap or soon to be one. Architecture is that great living creative spirit. . . ."

CARY JAMES

Mill Valley, California

❖ ACKNOWLEDGMENT ❖

The author and the publishers gratefully acknowledge the generous cooperation of the Imperial Hotel of Tokyo in making this publication possible.

❖ **INTRODUCTION** ❖

SURROUNDED by the rush and clangor of Tokyo, standing amidst the noise and the crowds of this immense and frantic city, is Frank Lloyd Wright's Imperial Hotel. Among new and shiny neighbors its age and disrepair assault the eye; faced all around by smooth and simple blocks, its intricacies of form and detail, of ornament and profile, confuse the onlooker searching for accustomed blandness. Once within, the grand complexity of plan piles up upon its image of ornate decay the frustration of spaces which demand the effort of involvement. In contrast to the anonymity of our usual public architecture whose purpose is to be that negative envelope which serves without influence, the Imperial will not let us drift through it untouched. But it is not our habit now to be involved with architecture, certainly not in the total way we must be with the Imperial; the impertinence of the building destroys the precarious balance of our lives; it wrings out of minds cut off from the world around, a recognition of the power and potency of the art of architecture. The swift buildings which shape our present cities do not demand this recognition and we remain comfortable among them, passing without contact and without memory through the vacuous shapes of function and impersonality, through these empty forms which stand as metaphors of our contemporary life. Soon the final hand of destruction will fall on the Imperial; the economic factors which lead in this direction, though deplorable, are at least understandable. But in fact, its destruction has already begun in the passive avoidance of its upkeep. Not yet fifty years old, the ruin of Wright's building bears witness to our distaste for the shape of his art and to his demand for our involvement. And to its rear rise the bland towers of the new section of the hotel, pointing to the future with rare precision.

The meaning of the Imperial must lie deeper than involvement. The foundations of its form must be more than a weakness for the ornate. Taste could not of itself have produced this great orchestrated being. The Imperial Hotel is the complex and enormous creation of an idea of art and life unique in the architecture of our time, indeed an idea found only rarely in our history. Frank Lloyd Wright stood outside the mainstream of Western culture. It is the foreignness of his thought which is behind the strangeness of all his architecture. His idea of man and the world were nearly opposite to ours; it is this we fail to grasp in our reaction to his art. To begin to understand Wright, it is necessary to put aside more of our traditional attitudes than may easily be done. It is necessary to see that his views of man and art were animated by the idea of unity, a sense of the singleness of all being and all life. This singleness, this interrelatedness shaped his mind and his architecture in unusual and to us often incomprehensible ways. It is unity which ordered the being of the Imperial Hotel. To understand the distance of this from our usual thought it is first necessary to look briefly at the framework of our own ideas of reality.

The structure of Western thought is analytic. To analyze is to abstract objects from reality, to isolate and to make static a being which began immersed in place and time. Analysis orders, catalogues; it deals with items as if they were abstract numerical values, fixed, unchanging, unaffected by time or place. Analysis deals with concepts, ideals, definitions, symbols—all of which remain true to inward static being, and are unaffected by objects outside themselves. The truth for which we search we conceive as static and as self-contained as the objects of our thought. Though the world we inhabit is shaped by time and interaction, we are convinced that its meaning lies behind in the simple, static order we have created in our heads, an order of symbol and of thought.

In architecture, analytic thought has emphasized shape and form as an ideal value, predetermined and static. The classic systems of columns and decoration became images of art; symbols of perfection applicable to any use, suited to any climate and any material. The changeless order of these aesthetic systems became the image of man separated from the world by his analytic mind, the creator of ideal beauty in the midst of violent, unfeeling chaos. Architecture became the physical creation which mirrored our philosophic search for simple-minded reconstructions of reality.

Analysis in thought and art thus does not deal with the actual being of the world, but with symbolic abstractions we have made of that world. We forget that the image we have created is not in fact the whole reality, and we find ourselves dealing with the world as if it were symbol and ideal. The nature of our concepts places great emphasis on the isolation of part to part, on the discreteness of phenomena, on the self-contained essence of all things. The world becomes a collection of static and precise objects; the meaning of the assemblage must be its arithmetical sum. And the order of the whole, because we have made its parts discrete and static and unaffected by time or relation, must be static and hierarchial in terms of position or dominance: either higher or lower, either for or against. This confrontation, this eternal dualism, has become our image of the world.

The admitted facility of analytic methods has culminated in the awesome power of contemporary science. This very success, however, has confirmed our belief in a world view which is narrow and artificial. The price we have paid for this success has distorted our whole culture. It is the unreconciled tension between mortal and divine which created and maintains the dogma of Christianity; it is the duality of the mental and the material and our insistence on the hierarchial primacy of mind which has shaped the eternal futility of philosophy as a balanced product of man. Even though science is now altering its direction, it is the idea of the isolation of the observer from his experiment and from his world which, in the mind of the scientist, continues his divorce from the moral and human questions of his work. When we place our faith in static abstraction and duality, and apply them to dynamic and interrelated men and societies—to living realities whose very meaning is relation and change—our impotence is total, and the results as evidenced in the human events of our time are catastrophic.

In the midst of this pervading cultural dualism, Frank Lloyd Wright attempted to reintroduce into architecture the opposite idea, the architecture of unity. In unity, all parts are vital and interworking members of the whole, and this relation is the root of life and of design. Meaning of parts arises out of relation as well as essence: the place of the part within the whole influences both part and whole. Unity deals with change and dynamism; objects and relations both change. The very nature of being and relation, which are both aspects of a single thing, is flux. In the broad terms of language, dualism emphasizes the thing, the noun; unity emphasizes the action, the verb.

Contemporary architecture, the radical change in forms of this century, has begun to move away from the analytic emphasis on form and aesthetics. It was Wright's master, Louis H. Sullivan, who first made popular the rallying cry, "form follows function," and began in his architecture to reverse the traditional emphasis on shape. Wright was himself one of the chief founders of the new movement; he seems to have been one of the few to realize the truly revolutionary nature of the new idea. Certainly Wright alone based his architecture on the unitary thought which is the ultimate consequence of that alteration of the dualistic tradition; he rephrased the original statement to: "form and function are one," a more accurate motto for the thought and architecture of unity.

The idea of unity sees the whole world and all its parts as single and integrate, immersed in life and time. Man and his buildings are intimate members of the single being of the world; out of this view comes the order and the being of the Imperial Hotel. Unity in architecture replaces static and preordained aesthetic form with a concern for the medium of use and reaction: space. Unity emphasizes the vital reality of the materials of construction rather than sacrificing them to the idea of shape. Unity insists that decoration be both unique and integral to architecture. And unity creates continuous, flexible, natural structure. It is not easy to see at first glance the low, massive bulk of the Imperial as shaped by the dynamics of becoming, but these consequences of unity illuminate the grand and difficult being which is this hotel.

The primary element in the Imperial, and in the architecture of Frank Lloyd Wright, is the space within the building. Space is the central reason for building; it is the useful volume within that is the generating element in architectural creation. But space is not just a void, not the absence of solids, not the hole left in the middle after the construction of the façades. Wright quoted Lao-tzu on space: "The reality of the building is the space within." Space was for Wright an invisible yet positive shape about which were placed the forms and materials of the building, a vital core which created the life and form of architecture. And further, in his thought there was no essential difference between inside and outside space: each were aspects of the greater single space of the world, space which architecture shapes and encloses for human purposes. The form of his buildings reflect this spatial interpenetration, this removal of distinction between exterior and interior, this singleness of space.

The concept of vigorous spatial reality results in the Imperial in a great orchestrated flow, alive in itself and taking life from the ornament and the materials around. It begins outside in the entrance court, where the long bedroom wings reach out past the pool to reshape this part of the city. Here is our introduction to this new idea of architecture; here in fact begins the space of the hotel. At the entrance the infinite ceiling of the sky is exchanged for the low roof of the porte-cochere, the space is firmly defined, and with this definition passes through the entry into the first business lobby. There it opens out again into a low wide place. The space becomes interior without abruptness or effort; there is a sense of arrival, of a positive place, of a created area contained but not bounded. There are many such places in the Imperial, yet the nature of the space is never static; always there are half-seen vistas, always eye and body are drawn through and up and beyond.

Up six or eight steps from this first lobby is the main lobby. Up from the first low overhead the space expands into a great three-storied volume, tall in relation to the horizontality of the hotel. At its corners great ornamented columns rise up past balconies and mezzanines to the roof, where banks of glazed doors bring light into the central core. Here again the flow of space slows and alters, and spreads out from this lobby in many interlocking layers, to sitting corners, into many-windowed lounges, onto the bright clerestoried dining room, and into corridors lined with glass doors that look out to central gardens, corridors which lead to the bedroom wings, or farther into the building. Here again is place without confinement, definition without immobility. And even in this ample volume it does not do to pause, for the spatial motion draws us on. The great flow, which began in the entrance court, continues up through this lobby and these corridors, past the dining room, up to the great cross-axis of the promenade beyond, and up and over a multitude of small dining rooms to the vast banquet hall over all. Even there no culmination exists, nor is there cessation in the movement, and through great glazed crossarms the space returns upon itself. This grand complex flow is the centerline of the hotel, yet at every turn it is possible to leave the major spaces for minor ones. There seems always to be another turning into a farther space; volumes interlock, and short runs of steps lead up to new outlooks. There are constantly changing perspectives of the interior, and through openings at unexpected places come views of the gardens and of the long bedroom wings.

To enter this hotel is to become involved in space whose very nature is limitless and unending: there is no certain point to be called beginning; there is no ending either. There is no self-centered progression of events and volumes leading to a long foreseen climax complete within itself. The shape of the Imperial's space is the shape of life; in all this complex motion there is neither tension nor confinement, and the strength and freedom of the space become ours as eye and body move. In the image of life, without origin and without end, unity in architecture has here created the integration of the physical building with the vital emptiness it encloses, and both with the greater void beyond. Space in the Imperial is part of a great continuum, a thing of constant becoming. It is space that is the heart of living architecture today.

As space is reinterpreted in this new sense of architecture, so too must be the making of the form of buildings. Materials are the means of construction: their weight and strength govern form and building method; their color and texture and size have profound influence on the experience of architecture. Traditional emphasis on form has often subjugated the properties of materials in the interest of aesthetic shape. The integrative concept of Wright's architecture recognizes materials themselves as affecting form and modifying space. This emphasis on matter brings architecture out of the abstract; the building is in itself reality.

In the Imperial Hotel the range of materials is limited and does not change significantly from exterior to interior. The major materials are brick and stone. Though plaster, wood, copper, and terra cotta are used, it is the texture of the brick and the patterned glory of the stone that create the hotel's warm reality.

Brick is the basic material: the maker of shape, it is form and facing for the structure of reinforced concrete. It is brown brick, on the exterior yellowish, on the interior dark; it is roughly lined with heavy scoring; it has the small variations of tone natural to baked clay. All these give emphasis to the texture of the masses; the eye is ever involved with the surface of the building. The mortar between the masonry is colored to match the brick. The vertical joints are brought flush and scored, the horizontal joints are deeply cut, and the masonry lies in long thin layers, its horizontality one with that of the hotel. On the interior these horizontal lines are painted with gold, its metallic glint contrasting warmly with the rough, brown brick, and in the dim far reaches of interior spaces this glitter gives definition to forms the brick is too dark to provide. The surface of the building, no longer bland and dull, creates life out of the nature of its materials, and this life is both shaped by and shapes the central living space. Materials participate in the architecture; the building becomes real and positive to hand and eye.

The use of brick emphasizes its expressive as well as its structural properties, but with the stone, expressiveness flowers into ornament. In the Imperial the stone is a light lava stone from Oya, easily cut and shaped. To work it Wright commanded abundant highly skilled labor, and it bears the infinite mark of his fertile imagination. The stone is everywhere, its very presence decorative, nearly every piece carved and patterned. It is accent and emphasis. It is transition between planes, between vertical and horizontal, between levels. It clarifies line and mass, it emphasizes change in form and enclosure, it blooms in great decorative bursts at piers and terminals. It is the base of walls, the rails of balconies. It is steps, the face of slabs, the capitals of columns. It is urns and brackets. It runs in strings of squares up fireplace fronts, up corners, along the ridges of the roof; it comes rippling down columns like so much ivy. Its shapes and patterns are numberless, from simple cubes and spheres to patterned lines, to great abstract statues. The volcanic origin of the stone gives it strong natural texture. The hand of the architect has overlaid all this with the patterns of exuberant geometry.

Yet behind the activity of this multitude of forms there is an order: as the building is itself a great complex geometric construction, thus the building's ornament partakes of the same geometry. As the structure is ordered on the warp and weft of the four-foot square, the basis of the decoration is the square related to the thickness of the brick and mortar course. Square and cubic shapes abound, not alone in stone. The first line of brick above the base is molded in a pattern of alternating squares; elsewhere there are other rectangular patterns which are both accents and perforated grilles. There are square units of terra cotta, both square and triangular internally, which are also accent and grille. Wherever there is glass, gold mosaic in a pattern of running squares is set into the glazing. In all of this, what most strikes the eye are the departures into triangles and spheres, spectacular exercises in decoration which even in their exuberance remain true to the system of geometric order. Geometry thus controls both the shape of the building and the order of the decoration, and in the Imperial Hotel each becomes inconceivable without the other. This is integral ornament, the decoration of integral building, a unity of thought and shape and use. This is ornament which has become an efflorescence organic to the reality of the architecture.

Underlying all these concerns is the need to support the building, the need for structure. In Wright's thought, unity, which reordered space and decoration and the use of materials, also remade structure, and it was the extension of this thought into the fabric of the building which preserved the hotel so well from the shock of earthquake. The hotel "floats" on the spongy mud of its site; the structure makes liberal use of cantilevers from central supports, reducing the danger of lateral displacement in supporting walls; the building is divided into numerous segments to provide controlled flexibility in seismic movement. Central to it all, out of unity arose continuous unified structure, an interrelation of parts more complex than the tradition of the upright and horizontal; in their knitting together a stronger and more economical building. The unscarred survival of the Imperial through the stress of earthquake demonstrates graphically the value of the idea of unity.

Yet structure integral to the building will order without dominating, for the demands of space and function are no less important than those of support.

Structure integral in architecture is a working part of the whole, neither beginning of design nor sole shaper of form. Thus structure in the Imperial appears as enclosure as often as support, and the unique systems which adapt the building to earthquake are seldom obvious.

The nature of this hotel is a great union of the multitude of the needs and forces which brought it into existence. We have considered it part by part. In union, emphasis is on the new whole which bringing together a multitude of parts creates. It is this sense of the whole, this interrelation of parts rather than the separate demonstration of the needs of each which is the idea of architecture in the Imperial Hotel. As Wright built it, all facets were integrated—from structure and materials and space and ornament, to furniture and carpets and lighting. Though the stain of time has obliterated much, evidences of Wright's work still remain to convince us of the living unity central to his thought, of the comprehensive effort required by unity in architecture. The hotel, with the men within and the world outside, was meant to be an entity single, integrate, and unitary.

Wright called his idea of unity "organic architecture": it is organic because the shapes of nature are unitary and related, and the sense of growth and singleness found in nature was to be the source for the forms of man. Man himself was to be no longer a separate precious entity, but an integrate part of the universe. For this reason Wright's buildings, as products of man unified with the earth, are intimately involved with the ground on which they stand. His first forms were born on the flat Midwest prairies of Chicago, where he saw the horizontal line as expressive of the needed integration of building and earth. This horizontality is still much evident in the forms of the Imperial; its relation to the ground was in strong contrast to that of its neighbors. In organic architecture, Wright meant the building to be "*of* the ground, not on it."

As the form of architecture associates with the ground, so too does its reality, space. In the Imperial we found no precise transition from interior to exterior. The space of the hotel is in fact the space of the city shaped for human use. Fortresses are no longer required against the world nor against the weather: our technology has made the first futile, the second foolish. Shelter rather than protection is the purpose of architecture. Man is free again to associate with the world, and the shape of architectural space reflects this union.

Organic architecture reaffirms the union of man and the natural environment. Nature, once seen as adversary and threat, now becomes origin and guide. The forces and shapes of life, the *principles* of structure and motion, the single order behind the innumerable forms—these become a source book for mind and eye. When Wright proposed the tree as ideal for the new American architecture, he was careful to add that it was not the physical shape of the tree he meant.

It is the principle of the life processes that the tree exhibits, and the clearest demonstration of the potential of these processes occurs where trees grow freely without crowding. Analogous to growth in nature, through the identity of life, is human development. Wright's architecture had its social basis in the concept of free, self-sustaining, self-reliant individuals, developing without misshaping restraint. Out of this arose his concern with the house as the architectural form dealing most intently with that small group of individuals which is the family. The purpose of organic architecture became the creation of an environment which would nurture the flowering of these individuals. His ideal city, Broadacre City, was a great diffusion of families upon the land at the density of an acre per person. Though agrarian in form, it was not essentially an escape to the soil. It was rather an attempt to reintegrate man with his natural origins, to free him of the strictures of an inorganic, dualistic culture by totally restructuring the civic order of that culture. It was an expression of his continuing search for an environment that would provide for every man the freedom and potential of growth Wright had found for himself on his country establishments in Wisconsin and Arizona.

In an age becoming increasingly urban and social, this rural individualism has seemed to many of his contemporaries the product of a bygone age. In the midst of reaction to Wright's social thought, the central idea of his art has been obscured. In a time when the other important makers of architecture have re-interpreted and re-emphasized the basic ideas of separateness which lie deep within our culture, an architecture of unity and relation has appeared romantic and unnecessary, and architects have failed to recognize the consequences of the dictum which reshaped their art. Emphasis on the equality of function and form replaces the will and whim of the designer with the order of natural processes integral to himself, his work, his world. It is upon these processes, these principles, this recognition of the singleness of the world, that Wright built. It is this unity of thought and action which shaped the Imperial Hotel; it is our failure of understanding which has doomed it.

Both the forms and the words of an architect spring from the same source, and an introduction to a building cannot exist without a parallel introduction to his writings. A number of quotations have been included from Wright's *An Autobiography,* which is perhaps the most accessible of the multitude of his writings. The shorter are found among the photographs; the longer are in a separate section.

The first of these longer quotes is an early statement of the principles of organic architecture. The phrasing emphasizes his concern with the American residence, for it was the radical reshaping of the house that was his first contribution to architecture. The form of that reshaping—the "Prairie Style"—is evident in transition in the Imperial Hotel.

The second quote is Wright's story of the design and building of the Imperial Hotel. The Japanese committee searching for an architect heard of him in Europe, and appeared at his home, Taliesin, in Wisconsin in 1915. From that time until 1922, the Imperial was the consuming effort of his life. Wright had always found affirmation for his ideas in Japanese art, especially the woodblock print. It could only have been gratifying to have been chosen by the Japanese for this major structure. The hotel, as organic response to the earthquake, was tested and proved decisively. Its nearly perfect survival vindicated his trials and confirmed his innovations. It gave dramatic demonstration to the accuracy of organic thought. For Wright the builder, few structures had more meaning.

It is obvious that these brief excerpts from Wright's voluminous writings can do no more than indicate the quality and strength of his thought. In a similar way, the photographs here can only imply without describing the reality of the hotel. For the camera eye is an abstraction of life; the seductive simplicity of its blacks and whites on plane surfaces must never be taken in themselves for what they portray. In architecture especially, the vibrant life and motion of space cannot be seen except by inference in the photograph, nor can the reality of color and its emotional impact be transmitted through the monochromatic picture. Our lives are lived in depth and color and immersed in time. The camera gives us an instantaneous, one-eyed, black-and-white image of that world. Its abstraction must always be kept in mind.

Our progress through any building, and especially through the myriad joys of the Imperial Hotel, consists necessarily of a complex succession of images, feelings, and reactions. The reality of our experience becomes the creative whole we make of all these things—the relation of our lives to environment, to art, and to motion through these in space and time. No book can substitute for the experience of architecture. This can only be, within the limits of word and photograph, an attempt to create here on paper a reality honestly related to the far greater reality of the Imperial Hotel. It is an effort to broaden our consideration and our understanding of not only this hotel, but the thought and the art of Frank Lloyd Wright.

❖ QUOTATIONS ❖

From "An Autobiography" by Frank Lloyd Wright

THE NEW HOUSE

As I had regularly gone to and fro between Oak Park and my work with Adler and Sullivan in Chicago, here at hand was the typical American dwelling, the 'monogoria' of earlier days, standing about on the Chicago prairie. That dwelling got there somehow and became typical. But by any faith in nature, implicit or explicit, it did not belong there. I had seen that far in the light of the conception of architecture as natural. And ideas had naturally begun to come to me as to a more natural house. Each house I built I longed for the chance to build another. And I soon got the chance. I was not the only one sick of hypocrisy and hungry for reality around there, I found.

What was the matter with the kind of house I found on the prairie? Well—let me tell you in more detail.

Just for a beginning, let's say that house *lied* about everything. It had no sense of Unity at all nor any such sense of space as should belong to a free man among a free people in a free country. It was stuck up and stuck on, however it might be done. Wherever it happened to be. To take any one of these so-called 'homes' away would have improved the landscape and cleared the atmosphere. It was a box, too, cut full of holes to let in light and air, an especially ugly one to get in and out of. Or else it was a clumsy gabled chunk of roofed masonry similarly treated. Otherwise joinery reigned supreme; you know—'Carpenter and Joiner,' it used to read on the signs. Floors were the only part of the house left plain and the housewife covered these with a tangled rug-collection, because otherwise the floors were 'bare'—bare, I suppose, only because one could not very well walk on jigsawing or turned spindles or plaster-ornament.

It is not too much to say that as an architect my lot in Oak Park was cast with an inebriate lot of sinners hardened by habit against every human significance except one—and why mention 'the one touch of nature that makes the whole world kin?' I will venture to say that the aggregation was the worst the world ever saw—at the lowest esthetic level in all history. Steam heat, plumbing and electric light were coming in as its only redeeming features.

My first feeling therefore had been a yearning for simplicity. A new sense of simplicity as 'organic.' This had barely begun to take shape in my mind when the Winslow house was planned. But now it began in practice. Organic simplicity might be seen producing significant character in the harmonious whole we call nature. Beauty in growing things. None were insignificant.

I loved the prairie by instinct as a great simplicity—the trees, flowers, sky itself, thrilling by contrast.

I saw that a little height on the prairie was enough to look like much more—every detail as to height becoming intensely significant, breadths all falling short. Here was tremendous spaciousness but all sacrificed needlessly. All space was cut up crosswise and cut up lengthwise into the fifty-foot lot—or would you have twenty-five feet less or twenty-five feet more? Salemanship cut and parceled it out, sold it with no restrictions. In a great, new, free country there was, then, everywhere a characteristic tendency to huddle and in consequence a mean tendency to tip everything in the way of human habitation up edgewise instead of letting it lie comfortably and naturally flat with the ground. Nor has this changed much since automobilization made it stupid as an economic measure and criminal as a social habit. I had an idea that the horizontal planes in buildings, those planes parallel to earth, identify themselves with the ground—make the building belong to the ground. I began putting this idea to work.

The buildings standing around there on the Chicago prairies were all tall and all tight. Chimneys were lean and taller still—sooty fingers threatening the sky. And beside them, sticking up almost as high, were the dormers. Dormers were elaborate devices—cunning little buildings complete in themselves—stuck on to the main roof-slopes to let the help poke their heads out of the attic for air. Invariably the damp, sticky clay of the prairie was dug out for a basement under the whole house and the rubble stone-walls of this dank basement always stuck above the ground a foot or so—and blinked through half-windows.

So the universal 'cellar' showed itself above ground as a bank of some kind of masonry running around the whole, for the house to sit on—like a chair. The lean upper house walls of the usual two floors above this stone or brick basement were wood and were set up on top of this masonry chair. Preferably house walls were both sided and shingled, mixed up and down or crosswise, together or with mouldings. These overdressed wood house walls had cut in them, or cut out of them to be precise, big holes for the big cat and little holes for the little cat to get in or get out or for ulterior purposes of light and air. These house walls were be-corniced or fancy-bracketed up at the top into the tall, purposely, profusely complicated roof. Dormers plus. The whole roof was ridged and tipped, swanked and gabled to madness before they would allow it to be either watershed or shelter. The whole exterior was be-deviled, that is to say, mixed to puzzle-pieces with corner-boards, panel-boards, window-frames, corner-blocks, plinth-blocks, rosettes, fantails, and jiggerwork in general. This was the only way 'they' seemed to have then of putting on style. The wood butchery of scroll-saw and turning lathe were at that moment the honest means to this fashionable and unholy but entirely moral end as things were.

Unless the householder of the period were poor indeed, usually the ingenious corner tower as seen in monogaria, eventuated into a candle-snuffer dome, a spire, an inverted rutabaga, radish or onion. Always elaborate bay-windows and fancy porches rallied around this imaginatively unimaginative corner fetich—ring around a rosie. And all this the builders of the period could do nearly as well in brick as in stone. It was an impartial society. All materials looked pretty much alike to it in that day and do today.

Simplicity was a far from this scrap-pile as the pandemonium of the barnyard is far from music. But easy for the architect. Oh yes. All he had to do was call, 'Boy, take down No. 37, and put a bay-window on it for the lady.'

BUILDING THE NEW HOUSE

First thing in building the new house, get rid of the attic, therefore the dormer. Get rid of the useless false heights below it. Next, get rid of the unwholesome basement, yes absolutely—in any house built on the prairie. Instead of lean, brick chimneys bristling up everywhere to hint at Judgment, I could see necessity for one chimney only. A broad generous one, or at most two. These kept low-down on gently sloping roofs or perhaps flat roofs. The big fireplace in the house below became now a place for a real fire. A real fireplace at that time was extraordinary. There were mantles instead. A mantle was a marble frame for a few coals in a grate. Or it was a piece of wooden furniture with tile stuck in it around the grate, the whole set slam up against the plastered, papered wall. Insult to comfort. So the *integral* fireplace became an important part of the building itself in the houses I was allowed to build out there on the prairie.

It comforted me to see the fire burning deep in the solid masonry of the house itself. A feeling that came to stay.

Taking a human being for my scale, I brought the whole house down in height to fit a normal one—ergo, $5'8\frac{1}{2}''$ tall, say. This is my own height. Believing in no other scale than the human being I broadened the mass out all I possible could to bring it down into spaciousness. It has been said that were I three inches taller than $5'8\frac{1}{2}''$ all my houses would have been quite different in proportion. Probably.

House walls were now started at the ground on a cement or stone water table that looked like a low platform under the building, and usually was. But the house walls were stopped at the second-story windowsill level to let the bedrooms come through above in a continuous window series below the broad eaves of a gentle sloping, overhanging roof. In this new house the wall was beginning to go as an impediment to outside light and air and beauty. Walls had been the great fact about the box in which holes had to be punched. It was still this conception of a wall-building which was with me when I designed the Winslow house. But after that my conception began to change.

My sense of 'wall' was no longer the side of a box. It was enclosure of space affording protection against storm or heat only when needed. But it was also to bring the outside world into the house and let the inside of the house go outside. In this sense I was working away at the wall as a wall and bringing it towards the function of a screen, a means of opening up space which, as control of building-materials improved, would finally permit the free use of the whole space without affecting the soundness of the structure.

The climate being what it was, violent in extremes of heat and cold, damp and dry, dark and bright, I gave broad protecting roof-shelter to the whole, getting back to the purpose for which the cornice was originally designed. The underside of roof-projections was flat and usually light in color to create a glow of reflected light that softly brightened the upper rooms. Overhangs had a double value: shelter and preservation for the walls of the house, as well as this diffusion of reflected light for the upper story through the 'light screens' that took the place of the walls and were now often the windows in long series.

And at this time I saw a house, primarily, as livable interior space under ample shelter. I liked the *sense of shelter* in the look of the building. I still like it. The house began to associate with the ground and become natural to its prairie site.

And would the young man in Architecture believe that this was all 'new' then? Yes—not only new, but destructive heresy—ridiculous eccentricity. All somewhat so today. Stranger still, but then it was *all* so *new* that what prospect I had of ever earning a livelihood by making houses was nearly wrecked. At first, 'they' called the houses 'dress reform' houses because Society was just then excited about that particular reform. This simplification looked like some kind of reform to the provincials.

What I have just described was on the *outside* of the house. But it was all there, chiefly because of what had happened *inside*.

Dwellings of that period were cut up, advisedly and completely, with the grim determination that should go with any cutting process. The interiors consisted of boxes beside boxes or inside boxes, called *rooms*. All boxes were inside a complicated outside boxing. Each domestic function was properly box to box.

I could see little sense in this inhibition, this cellular sequestration that implied ancestors familiar with penal institutions, except for the privacy of bedrooms on the upper floor. They were perhaps all right as sleeping boxes. So I declared the whole lower floor as one room, cutting off the kitchen as a laboratory, putting the servants' sleeping and living quarters next to the kitchen but semi-detached, on the ground floor. Then I screened various portions of the big room for certain domestic purposes like dining, reading, receiving callers.

There were no plans in existence like these at the time. But my clients were all pushed toward these ideas as helpful to a solution of the vexed servant problem. Scores of unnecessary doors disappeared and no end of partition. Both clients and servants liked the new freedom. The house became more free as space and more livable too. Interior spaciousness began to dawn.

Thus came an end to the cluttered house. Fewer doors; fewer window holes though much greater window area; windows and doors lowered to convenient human heights. These changes once made, the ceilings of the rooms could be brought down over on to the walls by way of the horizontal broad bands of plaster on the walls themselves above the windows and colored the same as the room-ceilings. This would bring ceiling-surface and color down to the very window tops. Ceilings thus expanded by way of the wall band above the windows gave generous overhead even to small rooms. The sense of the whole broadened, made plastic by this means.

Here entered the important new element of plasticity—as I saw it. And I saw it as indispensible element to the successful use of the machine. The windows would sometimes be wrapped around the building corners as inside emphasis of plasticity and to increase the sense of interior space. I fought for outswinging windows because the casement window associated house with the out-of-doors gave free openings outward. In other words, the so-called casement was not only simple but more human in use and effect. So more natural. If it had not existed I should have invented it. But it was not used at that time in the United States so I lost many clients because I insisted upon it. The client usually wanted the double-hung (the guillotine window) in use then, although it was neither simple nor human. It was only expedient. I used it once, in the Winslow house, and rejected it forever after. Nor at that time did I entirely eliminate the wooden trim. I did make the 'trim' plastic, that is to say, light and continuously flowing instead of the prevailing heavy 'cut and butt' carpenter work. No longer did trim, so called, look like carpenter work. The machine could do it all perfectly well as I laid it out, in this search for quiet. This plastic trim enabled poor workmanship to be concealed. There was need of that much trim then to conceal much in the way of craftsmanship because the battle between the machines and the Union had already begun to demoralize workmen.

Machine-resources of this period were so little understood that extensive drawings had to be made merely to show the mill-man what to leave off. Not alone in the trim but in numerous ways too tedious to describe in words, this revolutionary sense of the *plastic* whole began to work more and more intelligently and have facinating unforseen consequences. Nearly everyone had endured the house of the period as long as possible, judging by the appreciation of the change. Here was an ideal of organic simplicity put to work, with historical consequences not only in this country but especially in the thought of the civilized world.

SIMPLICITY

Organic simplicity—in this early constructive effort—I soon found depended upon the sympathy with which such co-ordination as I have described might be effected. Plainness was not necessarily simplicity. That was evident. Crude furniture of the Roycroft-Stickley-Mission style, which came along later, was offensively plain, plain as a barn door—but never simple in any true sense. Nor, I found, were merely machine-made things in themselves necessarily simple. 'To think,' as the Master used to say, 'is to deal in simples.' And this means with an eye single to the altogether.

This is, I believe, the single secret of simplicity: that we may truly regard nothing at all as simple in itself. I believe that no one thing in itself is ever so, but must achieve simplicity—as an artist should use the term—as a perfectly realized part of some organic whole. Only as a feature or any part becomes harmonious element in the harmonious whole does it arrive at the state of simplicity. Any wild flower is truly simple but double the same wildflower by cultivation and it ceases to be so. The scheme of the original is no longer clear. Clarity of design and perfect significance both are essentials of the spontaneous born simplicity of the lilies of the field. 'They toil not, neither do they spin.' Jesus wrote the supreme essay on simplicity in this, 'Consider the lilies of the field.'

Five lines where three are enough is always stupidity. Nine pounds where three are sufficient is obesity. But to eliminate expressive words in speaking or writing—words that intensify or vivify meaning is not simplicity. Nor is similar elimination in architecture simplicity. It may be, and usually is, stupidity.

In architecture, expressive changes of surface, emphasis of line and especially textures of material or imaginative pattern, may go to make facts more eloquent—forms more significant. Elimination, therefore, may be just as meaningless as elaboration, perhaps more often is so. To know what to leave out and what to put in; just where and just how, ah, *that* is to have been educated in knowledge of simplicity —toward ultimate freedom of expression.

As for objects of art in the house, even in that early day they were betes noires of the new simplicity. If well chosen, all right. But only if each were properly digested by the whole. Antique or modern sculpture, paintings, pottery, might well enough become objectives in the architectural scheme. And I accepted them, aimed at them often but assimilated them. Such precious things may often take their places as elements in the design of any house, be gracious and good to live with. But such assimilation is extraordinarily difficult. Better in general to design all as integral features.

I tried to make my clients see that furniture and furnishings that were not built in as integral features of the building should be designed as attributes to whatever furniture *was* built in and should be seen as a minor part of the building itself even if detached or kept aside to be employed only on occasions.

But when the building itself was finished the old furniture they already possessed usually went in with the clients to await the time when the interior might be completed in this sense. Very few of the houses, therefore, were anything but painful to me after the clients brought in their belongings.

Soon I found it difficult, anyway, to make some of the furniture in the abstract. That is, to design it as architecture and make it human at the same time—fit for human use. I have been black and blue in some spot, somewhere, almost all my life from too intimate contact with my own early furniture.

Human beings must group, sit or recline, confound them, and they must dine —but dining is much easier to manage and always a great artistic opportunity. Arrangements for the informality of sitting in comfort singly or in groups still belonging in disarray to the scheme as a whole: *that* is a matter difficult to accomplish. But it can be done now and should be done, because only those attributes of human comfort and convenience should be in order which belong to the whole in this modern integrated sense.

Human use and comfort should not be taxed to pay dividends on any designer's idiosyncrasy. Human use and comfort should have intimate possession of every interior—should be felt in every exterior. Decoration is intended to make more charming and comfort more appropriate, or else a privilege has been abused.

As these ideals worked away from house to house, finally freedom of floor space and elimination of useless heights worked a miracle in the new dwelling place. A sense of appropriate freedom had changed its whole aspect. The whole became different but more fit for human habitation and more natural to its site. It was impossible to imagine a house once built on these principles somewhere else. An entirely new sense of space-values in architecture came home. It now appears these new values came into the architecture of the world. New sense of repose in quiet streamline effects had arrived. The streamline and the plain surface seen as the flat plane had then and there, some thirty-seven years ago, found their way into buildings as we see them in steamships, aeroplanes and motorcars, although they were intimately to building materials, environment and the human being.

But, more important than all beside, still rising to greater dignity as an idea as it goes on working, was the ideal of plasticity. That ideal now began to emerge as a means to achieve an organic architecture.

PLASTICITY

Plasticity may be seen in the expressive flesh-covering of the skeleton as contrasted with the articulation of the skeleton itself. If form really 'followed function'—as the Master declared—here was the direct means of expression of the more spiritual idea that form and function are one: the only true means I could see then or can see now to eliminate the separation and complication of cut-and-butt joinery in favor of the expressive flow of continuous surface. Here, by instinct at first—all ideas germinate —a principle entered into building that has since gone developing. In my work the idea of plasticity may now be seen as the element of continuity.

In architecture, plasticity is only the modern expression of an ancient thought. But the thought taken into structure and throughout human affairs will re-create in a badly 'disjointed,' distracted world the entire fabric of human society. This magic word 'plastic' was a word Louis Sullivan himself was fond of using in reference to his idea of ornamentation as distinguished from all other or applied ornament. But now, why not the larger application in the structure of the building itself in this sense?

Why a principle working in the part if not living in the whole?

If form really followed function—it did in a material sense by means of this ideal of plasticity, the spiritual concept of *form and function as one*—why not throw away the implications of post or upright and beam or horizontal entirely? Have no beams or columns piling up as 'joinery.' Nor any cornices. Nor any 'features' as *fixtures*. No. Have no appliances of any kind at all, such as pilasters, entablatures and cornices. Nor put into the building any fixtures whatsoever as 'fixtures.' Eliminate the separations and separate joints. Classic architecture was all fixation-of-the-fixture. Yes, entirely so. Now why not let walls, ceilings, floors become *seen* as component parts of each other, their surfaces flowing into each other. To get continuity in the whole, eliminating all constructed features just as Louis Sullivan had eliminated background in his ornament in favor of an integral sense of the whole. Here the promotion of an idea from the material to the spiritual plane began to have consequences. Conceive now that an entire building might grow up out of conditions as a plant grows up out of soil and yet be free to be itself, to 'live its own life according to Man's Nature.' Dignified as a tree in the midst of nature but a child of the spirit of man.

I now propose an ideal for the architecture of the machine age, for the ideal American building. Let it grow up in that image. The tree.

But I do not mean to suggest the imitation of the tree.

Proceeding, then, step by step from generals to particulars, plasticity as a large means in architecture began to grip me and to work its own will. Fascinated I would watch its sequences, seeing other sequences in those consequences already in evidence: as in the Heurtley, Martin, Heath, Thomas, Tomek, Coonley and dozens of other houses.

The old architecture, so far as its grammar went, for me began, literally, to disappear. As if by magic new architectural effects came to life—effects genuinely new in the whole cycle of architecture owing simply to the working of this spiritual principle. Vistas of inevitable simplicity and ineffable harmonies would open, so beautiful to me that I was not only delighted, but often startled. Yes, sometimes amazed.

I have since concentrated on plasticity as physical continuity, using it as a practical working principle within the very nature of the building itself in an effort to accomplish this great thing called architecture. Every true esthetic is an implication of nature, so it was inevitable that this esthetic ideal should be found to enter into the actual building of the building itself as a principle of construction.

But later on I found that in the effort to actually eliminate that post and beam in favor of structural continuity, that is to say, making the two things one thing instead of two separate things, I could get no help from regular engineers. By habit, the engineer reduced everything in the field of calculation to the post and the beam resting upon it before he could calculate and tell you where and just how much for either. He had not other data. Walls made one with floors and ceilings, merging together yet reacting upon each other, the engineer hand never met. And the engineer had not yet enough scientific formulae to enable him to calculate for continuity.

Floor slabs and extended as cantilevers over centered supports, as a waiter's tray rests upon his upturned fingers, such as I now began to use in order to get planes parallel to the earth to emphasize the third dimension, were new, as I used them, especially in the Imperial Hotel. But the engineer soon mastered the element of continuity in floor slabs, with such formulae as he had. The cantilever thus became a new feature of design in architecture. As used in the Imperial Hotel in Tokio it was the most important of the features of construction that insured the life of that building in the terrific temblor of 1922. So, not only a new esthetic but proving the esthetic as scientifically sound, a great new economic 'stability' derived from steel in tension was able now to enter into building construction.

The Nature of Materials

From this early ideal of plasticity another concept came. To be consistent in practice, or indeed if as a principle it was to work out in the field at all, I found that plasticity must have a new sense, as well as a science of materials. The greatest of the materials, steel, glass, ferro- or armored concrete were new. Had they existed in the ancient order we never would have had anything at all like 'classic architecture.'

And it may interest you, as it astonished me, to learn that there was nothing in the literature of the civilized world on the nature of materials in this sense. So I began to study the nature of materials, learning to *see* them. I now learned to see brick as brick, to see wood as wood, and to see concrete or glass or metal. See each for itself and all as themselves. Strange to say, this required greater concentration of imagination. Each material demanded different handling and had possibilities peculiar to its own nature. Appropriate designs for one material would not be appropriate at all for another material. At least, not in the light of this spiritual ideal of simplicity as *organic plasticity*. Of course, as I could now see, there could be no organic architecture where the nature of materials was ignored or misunderstood. How could there be? Perfect correlation is the first principle of growth. Integration, or even the very word 'organic' means that nothing is of value except as it is naturally related to the whole in the direction of some living purpose, a true part of entity. My old master had designed for all the old materials all alike; brick, stone, wood, iron wrought or iron cast, or plaster—all were grist for his rich imagination and his sentient ornament.

To him all materials were only one material in which to weave the stuff of his dreams. I still remember being ashamed of the delight I took at first thus seeing—thanks to him too—so plainly around the beloved Master's own practice. But *acting* upon this new train of ideals brought work sharply up against the tool I could find to get the ideas in practical form: the Machine. What were the tools in use everywhere? Machines—automatic, most of them. Stone- or wood-planers, molding shapers, various lathes and power saws, all in commercialized organized mills. Sheet-metal breakers, gigantic presses, shears, molding and stamping machines in the sheet metal industry, commercialized in 'shops.' Foundaries and rolling-mills turned out cast-iron and steel in any imaginable shape. The machine as such had not seemed to interest Louis Sullivan. Perhaps he took it for granted. But what a resource, that rolling or drawing or extruding of metal! And more confusion to the old order, concrete-mixers, form-makers, clay-bakers, casters, glass-makers, all in organized trade unions.

And the unions themselves were all units in a more or less highly commercialized union in which craftsmanship had no place except as survival-for-burial. Standardization had already become an inflexible necessity. Standardization was either the enemy or a friend to the architect. He might choose. But I felt that as he chose he became master and useful or else he became a luxury and eventually a parasite. Although not realized then at all nor yet completely realized by the architect, machine standardization had already taken the life of handicraft in all its expressions. If I was to realize new buildings I should have to have new technique. I should have to so design buildings that they would not only be appropriate to materials but design them so the machine that would *have* to make them could make them surpassingly well. By now, you see, I had come under the discipline of a great ideal. There is no discipline so severe as the perfect integration of true correlation in any human endeavor. But there is no discipline that yields such rich rewards in work, nor is there any discipline so safe and sure of results. (Why should human relations be excepted?) The straight line, the flat plane were limitations until proved benefits by the Machine. But steel-in-tension was clearly liberation.

*   *   *   *   *

BUILDING AGAINST DOOMSDAY

WHY THE GREAT EARTHQUAKE DID NOT DESTROY THE IMPERIAL HOTEL

From infancy, a sort of subjective contemplation, the minds and hearts of the Japanese are fixed upon the great calm mountain God of their nation—the sacred Fuji-yama brooding in majesty and eternal calm over all. They deeply worship as the mountain continually changes moods, combining with sun and moon, clouds and mist in a vast expression of elemental beauty the like of which in dignity and repose exists nowhere else on earth.

It is not too much to say that the sacred mountain is the God of old Japan; Japan the Modern Ancient.

And yet the dreaded force that made the great mountain, continually takes its toll of life from this devoted people, as the enormous weight of the deep sea beside the tenuous island, the deepest sea in the world, strains the earth-crust, opening fissures in the bottom of the great valley in which it rests and the sea rushes down to eternal fires to become gas and steam expanding or exploding internally, causing earth convulsions that betray the life on the green surface. Great wave movements go shuddering through the body of their land, spasmodically changing all overnight in immense areas. Whole villages disappear. New islands appear as others are lost and all with them. Shores are reversed as mountains are laid low and valleys are lifted up. And always flames! The terror of it all invariably faces conflagration at the end.

Trained by these disasters of the centuries to build lightly on the ground—the wood and paper houses natural to them may be kindled by any spark. When fire starts it seldom stops short of several hundred homes and usually thousands, or complete destruction. So, when the earthquake is violent, fire finishes the terrible work.

The dead not swallowed up, are buried, and once more *Shikata-ga-nai* (it cannot be helped) goes patiently on as before. Naturally the earth-waves seem fate and unconquerable. A force useless to combat in strength alone, for it is mightier than any force at man's command. *Shikata-ga-nai*! This stoicism I have seen and lived with four years or more while preparing to meet this awful force by building on ground which the seismograph shows is never for a moment still—prepare to meet it by other means than rigid force.

The foreigner with the advent of Commodore Perry came to share Japanese joys and sorrows, and soon a building was needed to shelter the foreign element of Tokio, the capital of Japan. A social clearing house became necessary to official Japan as a consequence of the new foreign interest in them, because, for one reason, no foreigner could live on the floor. The need steadily increased. At that time the Mikado took it upon himself to meet the need, and asked the Germans to build one of their characteristic national wood and plaster extravaganzas for the purpose.

That wretched marvel grew obsolete and the need of another, a great one, imperative. The Imperial Household, this time, proposed to share the task of providing the new accommodation with the capitalists of the Empire, shipowners, cement manufacturers, bankers, tobacco interests, etc., and I, an American, was chosen to do the work.

No foreigner yet invited to Japan had taken off his hat to Japanese traditions. When foreigners came, what they had back home came too, suitable or not, and the politely humble Japanese, duly impressed, took the offering and marveled. They tried to do likewise in their turn. And yet Japanese fine-art traditions are among the noblest and purest in this world, giving Chinese origins due credit. It was my instinct not to insult them. The West has much to learn from the East—and Japan was the gateway to that great East of which I had been dreaming since I had seen my first Japanese prints—and read my first Laotze.

But this terrible natural enemy to all building whatsoever—the temblor!

The terror of the temblor never left me while I planned the building nor while, more than four years, I worked upon it. Nor is anyone allowed to forget it—sometimes awakened at night by strange sensations as at sea, strangely unearthly and yet rumbling earth-noises. Sudden shocks, subsidence—and swinging. Again shock after shock and upheaval, jolting back and swinging. A sense of the bottom falling from beneath the building, terror of the coming moments as cracking plaster and groaning timbers indicate the whole structure may come crashing and tumbling down. There may be more awful threat to human happiness than earthquake. I do not know what it can be.

The Japanese turn livid, perspiration starts on them, but no other sign unless the violence becomes extreme, then—panic. I studied the temblor. Found it a wave-movement, not of sea but of earth—accompanied by terrific shocks no rigidity could withstand.

Because of the wave movements, deep foundations like long piles would oscillate and rock the structure. Therefore the foundation should be short or shallow. There was sixty to seventy feet of soft mud below the upper depth of eight feet of surface soil on the site. That mud seemed a merciful provision—a good cushion to relieve the terrible shocks. Why not float the building upon it? A battleship floats on salt water. And why not extreme lightness combined with tenuity and flexibility instead of the great weight necessary to the greatest possible rigidity? Why not, then, a building made as two hands thrust together palms inward, fingers interlocking and yielding to movement—but resilient to return to original position when distortion ceased? A flexure—flexing and reflexing in any direction. Why fight the quake? Why not sympathize with it and out-wit it?

That was how the building began to be planned.

The most serious problem was how to get the most carrying power out of that eight feet of cheese-like soil that overlay the liquid mud. During the first year of plan-making, I made borings nine inches in diameter eight feet deep and filled them with concrete. Arranged to test the concrete pins thus made. Got carloads of pig iron and loaded the pins until they would drive into the ground. Kept the test figures of loads and reactions. Took borings all over the site to find soft pockets. Water stood in the holes two feet below the surface, so the concrete had to go in quickly as the borings were completed. Later, tapered piles were driven in to *punch* the holes and pulled out—the concrete thrown directly in as the pile was out of the way.

These data in hand, the foundation plan was made to push these concrete pins two feet on centers each way over the entire areas on which the wall footings were to spread. The strength of the whole depth of eight feet of top soil was thus brought to bear at the surface. That was simple. But here was a compressible soil that might take a squeeze under the broad footings to add to the friction of the pins. Experiments showed the squeeze could safely be added to the friction. This meant a settlement of the building of five inches, the building itself driving the piles that much deeper. This was economy, but dangerous and more complicated.

But finally the building was computed pound by pound and distributed according to test data to 'float' below the grade of the ground surface—and it did. With some few slight variations it stayed there.

This foundation saved hundreds of thousands of dollars over the foundations then in use in Tokio. But had the owners of the Imperial superficially known what was contemplated something might have happened to prevent it. Rumor nearly did prevent it. Here, however, was the desired shock-absorber, a cushion, pins and all, to be uniformly loaded and put to work against the day of reckoning.

Now how to make the flexible structure instead of the foolish rigid one? Divide the building into parts. Where the parts were necessarily more than sixty feet long, joint these parts clear through floors, walls, footings and all, and manage the joints in the design. Wherever part met part, through joints also. So far, good sense, and careful calculation.

But a construction was needed where floors would not be carried between walls, because subterranean disturbances might move the walls and drop the floors. Why not then carry the floors as a waiter carries his tray on upraised arm and fingers at the center—*balancing* the load? All supports centered under the floor slabs like that instead of resting the slabs on the walls at their edges as is usually the case?

This meant the cantilever, as I had found by now. The cantilever is most romantic, most free, of all principles of construction, and in this case it seemed the most sensible. The waiter's tray supported by his hand at the center is a cantilever slab in principle. And so concrete cantilever slabs continuous across the building from side to side, supported in that way, became the structure of the Imperial Hotel at Tokio.

Roof tiles of Japanese buildings have murdered countless thousands of Japanese in upheavals, so a light hand-worked green copper roof was planned. Why kill more?

The outer walls were spread wide, thick and heavy at the base, growing thinner and lighter toward the top. Whereas Tokio buildings were all top-heavy. The center of gravity was kept low against the swinging movements and the slopes were made an esthetic feature of the design. The outside cover-hangs of the cantilever slabs where they came through the walls were all lightened by ornamental perforations enriching the light and shade of the structure. The stone everywhere under foot in Tokio was a workable light lava weighing as much as green oak. It was considered sacrilege to use this common material for the aristocratic edifice. But finally it was used for the feature material and readily yielded to any sense of form the architect might choose to indicate. And the whole structure was to be set up as a double shell—two shells, an exterior of slim cunning bricks, and an interior one of fluted hollow bricks raised together to a convenient height of four feet or more. The shells were to be poured solid with concrete to bind them together.

The great building thus became a jointed monolith with a mosaic surface of lava and brick. Earthquakes had always torn piping and wiring apart where laid in the structure and had flooded or charged the building. So all piping and wiring was to be laid free of construction in covered concrete trenches in the ground of the basements, independent even of foundations. Mains and all pipes were of lead with wiped joints, the lead bends sweeping from the trenches to be hung free in vertical pipe shafts, from which the curved lead branches were taken off, curved, to the stacks of bathrooms. Thus any disturbance might flex and rattle but not break the pipes or wiring.

Last but not least there was to be an immense reservoir or pool as an architectural feature of the entrance court—connected to the water system of the hotel and conserving the roof water.

Thus the plans were made so that all architectural features were practical necessities, and the straight line and flat plane were respectively modified in point of style to a building bowing to the traditions of the people to whom the building would belong. The *nature* of the design too, I wanted to make something their intensive hand methods could do well, because we didn't know what machinery could be used. It was impossible to say how far we could go with that. Probably not very far.

Finally the plans were ready.

No estimates could be had. It was all so unfamiliar, no commercial concern would touch it. Nothing left but to abandon the whole or organize to build it ourselves. The Imperial Hotel and its architect and builder. The language was a barrier. The men and methods strange.

But the foreign architect—with eighteen or twenty architectural students from the Japanese universities, several of whom were taken to Wisconsin during the plan-making period—and one expert foreign builder, Paul Mueller of Chicago, two foreigners, all else native, we organized with the hotel manager, Hayashi-San, as general manager. We had already bought pottery kilns in Shizuoka and made the long cunning bricks, of a style and size never made before for the outside shell. They were now ready to use. We had also made the fluted hollow bricks for the inside shell, the first in the Empire. We bought a fine lava-quarry at Oya near Nikko for the feature-material and started a flood of dimension stone moving down to the site in Tokio—a stream that kept piling into the building for four years. The size of the hole left in the ground at Oya was about like the excavations for the Grand Central Terminal.

We had a hundred or more clever stone choppers beating out patterns of the building on the greenish, leopard-spotted lava, for that period. On an average we employed about 600 men continually for four years. As a large proportion of them came from the surrounding country they lived round about in the building as we built it. With their numerous families, there they were—cooking, washing, sleeping. And we tried faithfully—sometimes frantically and often profanely—to teach them to build it, halfway between our way and their way.

We tried the stone-planner with the stone cutters. It was soon buried beneath the chips that flew from their busy stone-axes. Tried derricks and gin-poles and hoists. They preferred to carry heavy loads and enormous stones up inclined planes on their shoulders. We tried to abolish scaffolding and teach them to lay brick from the inside. Not to be done. They lashed tapering poles together in cunning ways as for centuries and clung with prehensile toes to the framework.

How skillful they were! What craftsmen! How patient and clever. So instead of wasting them by vainly trying to make them come our way—we went with them their way. I modified many original intentions to make the most of what I now saw was naturally theirs. The language grew less an obstruction. But curious mistakes were perpetual. It is true that the Japanese approach to any matter is a spiral. Their instinct for attack in any direction is oblique and volute. But they make up for it in gentleness and cleverness and loyalty. Yes, the loyalty of the retainer to his *Samurai*. They soon educated us and all went pretty well.

The countenance of the building began to emerge from the seemingly hopeless confusion of the enormous area now covered by the building materials of its terraces and courts and hundreds of families. And the workmen grew more and more interested in it. It was no uncommon thing to see groups of them admiring and criticizing too as some finished portion would emerge—criticizing intelligently.

There was a warmth of appreciation and loyalty unknown in the building circles of our country. A fine thing to have experienced.

The curse of the work was the holiday. There were no Sundays, but a couple of holidays every fortnight instead, and it took a day or two to recover from most of them. So the work dragged. And the rainy season! The Japanese say it rains up from the ground as well as down from the sky—in Tokio. We did succeed in abolishing the expensive cover-shed of tight roof and hanging matting sides under which most buildings are built in Japan. We congratulated ourselves until we found they knew their climate better than we did. Had we protected them from the rain and the burning sun the buildings would have been finished about seven months sooner—besides making all more comfortable and so more efficient.

A few more such "successes" would have been enough.

The directors met regularly for a couple of years and began to complain.

Rumors reached them from the English (the English love the Americans in Tokio) and Americans (why are Americans invariably so unpleasant to one another abroad?) to the effect that the architect of their building was mad. In any earthquake the whole thing would tumble apart—and the whole building would sink out of sight in the mud beneath. There was room enough for it in that cushion of mud. Where all had been pleasant enthusiasm, things began to drag. The loyalty of my own office force never for a moment wavered, but manager Hayashi was daily hectored and censured. At this crucial time it became apparent that three and a half million yen more would be necessary to complete and finish the work. Things looked dark.

By now a small army was working away in the lower stories of the building as it was completed. As soon as one portion was built it became a hive of frantic industry. The copper features and fixtures and roof tiles were all made there; the interior woodwork and furniture—the upholstery and many other things went on in the vast interior spaces as soon as the floor slabs covered them over.

I had brought examples of good furniture from home and took them apart to teach the Japanese workmen how to make them according to new designs which made them all part of the structure. They were fine craftsmen at this. Rug designs had gone to Pekin. The rugs were being woven there to harmonize with the interior features of the great rooms and the guest rooms. We were about two-thirds of the way over with the building itself. The foreigners had no way of keeping track of costs or finding out much about them in detail. So things had gone on for several years.

The crash came.

The directors were called together.

Baron Okura was chairman of the board—representing his own interests, the interest of the Imperial Royal Household, sixty percent, besides ownership of the ground. There was also Asano-San—a white-haired Samson of the shipping interests —a powerful man with shaggy white brows and piercing eyes. Murai of the tobacco interests—a peacemaker, with pleasant ways always. Wakai, the banker, as broad as he was long, with a beard that reached below the table when he stood up. Kanaka, a half dozen others.

Baron Okura had rather sponsored me from the beginning. He was in trouble now. The meetings had been held in the old hotel building and were pleasant social affairs with refreshments. This one was not. It looked black. A long time, it had been threatening. The Baron, a black-haired youth of eighty—a remarkable man regarded as one of the astute financial powers of the Empire—sat at the head of the table. I sat on his left. On his right sat his cultivated secretary, a Harvard graduate, who was interpreter. It doesn't matter where the others were. They were there and all talking at once. I answered the leading questions without end. The foundations. Always the foundations—and the money. The money!

The Baron was patient and polite—for some time. His lower lip had a trick of sticking out and quivering when he became intense. The personal idiosyncrasy of his was evident now. Suddenly he rose—leaned forward, head thrust forward, angry, hissing, pounding the table with both fists—extraordinary conduct for him.

The crowd went back and down as though blown down by the wind.

There was silence—the Baron still standing looking over toward me. Not knowing what it was all about I instinctively rose. The interpreter rose, too, and said, 'The Baron says that if the "young man" (all things are relative) will himself remain in Japan until the building is finished, he the Baron will himself find the necessary money and they could all go to—' whatever the Japanese word is for the place they could go to.

Although homesick by now and sick besides I reached out my hand to the Baron. The compact was made. The meeting was over. The directors filed out, red and angry to a man, instead of happy to have the responsibility lifted from them.

Was it Pericles who enacted some such role as the Baron's when the Parthenon was building? Anyway, the building of the new Imperial went on. Now every director became a spy. The walls had ears. Propaganda increased. My freedom was gone. I worked under greater difficulties than ever. But my little band of Japanese apprentices was loyal and we got ahead until another storm broke.

'Why not,' said the directors to the Baron, 'eliminate the pool and save 40,000 yen?' The Baron saw sense in this and sent for me. His mind was made up. No arguments took effect. I told him via interpreters that it was the last resource against the quake. In disaster, the city water would be cut off, and the window frames being wood in the 500-foot building front along the side street where wooden buildings stood, fire could gut the structure even though it withstood the quake. I had witnessed five terrible fires in Tokio already—walls of flame nothing in any degree inflammable could withstand.

No matter. The pool must come out. No. I said, it is wrong to take it out, and by such interference he would release me from my agreement and I could and would go home with no further delay. And I left his office. But I did not leave Tokio and the pool went in to play its final part in the great drama of destruction that followed two years later.

Another year and I could go home. The Tokio climate, so moist and humid summer and winter, depressing except in fall and early spring, together with the work and anxiety were wearing me down.

But now came a terrible test that calmed troublesome fears and made the architect's position easier.

The building construction was about finished. The architect's work-room had been moved to the top of the left wing above the promenade entrance. It was nearly noon. The boys in the office, reduced to ten, were there, and workmen were about. Suddenly with no warning a gigantic jolt lifted the whole building, threw the boys down sprawling with their drawing boards. A moment's panic and hell broke loose as the wave motions began. The structure was literally in convulsions. I was knocked down by the rush of workmen and my own boys to save their own lives. It is a mercy there were not more workmen in the roof space beyond, or I should have been trampled out. As I lay there I could clearly see the ground swell pass through the construction above as it heaved and groaned to hideous crushing and grinding noises. Several thunderous crashes sickened me, but later these proved to be the falling of five tall chimneys of the old Imperial, left standing alone by the recent burning of that building.

At the time it seemed as though the banquet hall section, invisible just beyond the work-room, had crashed down.

Only one faithful assistant stayed through this terrible ordeal. Endo-San, loyal right-bower—white to the teeth—perspiring. Otherwise the building was utterly deserted. We got up shaking to the knees and went together out onto the roofs. There across the street were crowds of frightened workmen. They had thrown down their tools and run for their lives, even those working in the courts. There they all stood strangely silent, pasty-faced, shaking. A strange silence too was everywhere over the city. Soon fires broke out in a dozen places. Bells rang and pandemonium broke. Women dragging frightened children ran weeping and wailing along the streets below.

We had just passed through the worst quake in fifty-two years. The building was undamaged. A transit put on the foundation levels showed no deviation whatever.

The work had been proved.

Hayashi-San, when reports of the damage to the city and none to the building came in, burst into tears of gratitude. His life had barely been worth living for more than a year, so cruel were the suspicions, so harassing the doubts. The year passed. The building was now so nearly complete there was no longer pressing need for the presence of the architect.

Another wing remained to be finished but it was a duplication of the one already done and furnished. So I could go home with good conscience. My clients, headed by the Baron, were generous, added substantial proof of appreciation to my fee, and I was 'farewelled' first at a champagne luncheon by the Baron and his directors; then at a tea house entertainment by the building organization itself, all with unique expressions of esteem; finally by the workmen after their no less generous fashion: Witness:

The day of sailing came. To get to my car I had to pass from the rear through the new building to the front. All was deserted and I wondered. Arrived at the entrance courts, there all the workmen were, crowding the spaces, watching and waiting. Already there had been gratifying evidence of appreciation—I thought— but here was the real thing. This could have happened nowhere but in Japan. Here was the spirit I had tried to compliment and respect in my work.

As their architect came out they crowded round, workmen of every rank from sweepers to foremen of 'the trades,' laughing, weeping, wanting awkwardly to shake hands—foreign fashion. They had learned 'aw-right,' and mingled it now with 'arigato' and 'sayonara Wrieto-San.'

Too much, and 'Wrieto-San' broke. They followed the car down along Hibiya way to the station, running, shouting, 'Banzai, Wrieto-San, banzai!'

The dock at Yokohama, eighteen miles away, was reached by train, to find that sixty of the foremen had paid their way down from Tokio to shout again and wave good-bye, while they faded from sight as the ship went down the bay. Such people! Where else in all the world would such touching warmth of kindness in faithfulness be probable or possible?

Two years later—1923—in Los Angeles. News of terrible disaster shouted in the streets. Tokio and Yokohama wiped out! The most terrible temblor of all history!

Appalling details came day after day. Nothing human, it seemed, could have withstood the cataclysm. Too anxious to get any sleep I tried to get news of the fate of the New Imperial, of Shugio, Endo, Hayashi-San, the Baron, and the host of friends I had left over there. Finally, the third night and about two in the morning the telephone bell rang. The *Examiner* wished to inform me that the Imperial Hotel was completely destroyed. My heart sank but I laughed, 'How do they *know?*' The night editor read the dispatch, a list of Imperial University, Imperial Theatre, Imperial Hospital, Imperial this and Imperial that.

'You see,' I said, 'how easy it is to get the Imperial Hotel mixed with the other Imperials? I am sure if anything is above ground in Tokio it is that building. If you print its destruction as "news" you will have to retract.'

Their turn to laugh and hang up the receiver. Ten days of uncertainty and conflicting reports, for during most of that time direct communication was cut off. Then a cablegram . . .

FRANK LLOYD WRIGHT
  OLIVE HILL STUDIO RESIDENCE B 1645 VERMONT AVE
  HOLLYWOOD CALIF
FOLLOWING WIRELESS RECEIVED FROM TOKIO TODAY
  HOTEL STANDS UNDAMAGED AS MONUMENT OF YOUR GENIUS
  HUNDREDS OF HOMELESS PROVIDED BY PERFECTLY MAINTAINED SERVICE
  CONGRATULATIONS (signed) OKURA IMPEHO

For once good news was news and the Baron's cablegram flashed around the world to herald the triumph of good sense. Both the great Tokio homes of the Baron were gone. The splendid museum he gave to Tokio and all its contents were destroyed. The building by the American architect, whose hand he took and whose cause he sponsored, was all he had left in Tokio—nor could love or money buy it now or buy a share of stock in it.

When the letters began to come in and nearly all the friends were found to be safe the news most gratifying to the architect was the fact that after the first great quake was over, the dead rotting there in unburied heaps, the Japanese in subsequent shocks coming in droves dragging their children into the courts and onto the terraces of the building, praying for protection by the God that has protected that building; then as the wall of fire, driving a great wail of human misery before it, came sweeping across the city toward the long front of the building, the hotel boys formed a bucket line to the big pool, the water there the only water available anywhere. And then kept the window sashes and frames on that side wet to meet the flames that came leaping across the narrow street.

The last thought for the safety of the New Imperial had taken effect.

All doctrines, all politics and civilization exurge from you,
All sculpture and monuments and anything inscribed anywhere are tallied in you,
The gist of histories and statistics as far back as the records reach is in you this hour—
and myths and tales the same;
If you were not breathing and walking here where would they all be?
The most renowned poems would be ashes . . . orations and plays would be vacuums.
All architecture is what you do to it when you look upon it;
Did you think it was in the white or gray stone? or the lines of the arches and cornices?

—WALT WHITMAN, *Leaves of Grass*

4

9

Architecture now becomes integral, the expression of a new-old reality: the livable interior space of the room itself. In integral architecture the *room-space itself must come through*. The *room* must be seen as architecture, or we have no architecture. We have no longer an outside as outside. We have no longer an outside and an inside as two separate things. Now the outside may come inside, and the inside may and does go outside. They are *of* each other. Form and function thus become one in design and execution if the nature of materials and method and purpose are all in unison.

This interior-space concept, the first broad integrity is the first great resource. It is also true basis for general significance of form. Add to this for the sake of clarity that (although the general integration is implied in the first integrity) it is in the nature of any organic building to grow from its site, come out of the ground into the light—the ground itself held always as a component basic part of the building itself. And then we have primarily the new ideal of building as organic. A building dignified as a tree in the midst of nature.

—FRANK LLOYD WRIGHT, *An Autobiography*

15

This dawning sense of the *Within* as *reality* when it is clearly seen as *Nature* will by way of glass make the garden be the building as much as the building will be the garden: the sky as treasured a feature of daily indoor life as the ground itself.

You may see that walls are vanishing. The cave for human dwelling purposes is at last disappearing.

—FRANK LLOYD WRIGHT, *An Autobiography*

19

. . . I began to study the nature of materials, learning to *see* them. I now learned to see brick as brick, to see wood as wood, and to see concrete or glass or metal. See each for itself and all as themselves. Strange to say, this required greater concentration of imagination. Each material demanded different handling and had possibilities of use peculiar to its own nature. Appropriate designs for one material would not be appropriate at all for another material. At least, not in the light of this spiritual ideal of simplicity as *organic plasticity*. Of course, as I could now see, there could be no organic architecture where the nature of materials was ignored or misunderstood. How could there be? Perfect correlation is the first principle of growth. Integration, or even the very word 'organic' means nothing is of value except as it is naturally related to the whole in the direction of living purpose, a true part of entity.

—FRANK LLOYD WRIGHT, *An Autobiography*

. . . integral ornament—the nature-pattern of actual construction. Here, confessed as the spiritual demand for true significance,
comes this subjective element in modern architecture. An element
so hard to understand that modern architects themselves seem to
understand it least well of all. . . . Ornament meaning not only
surface qualified by human imagination but imagination giving *natural
pattern* to structure. . . . Integral ornament is simply *structure-
pattern made visibly articulate* and seen in the building as it is seen
articulate in the structure of the trees or a lily of the fields. It is
the expression of inner rhythm of Form. Are we talking about
Style? Pretty nearly. At any rate we are talking about the qualities
that make *essential architecture* as distinguished from any mere act
of building whatsoever.

—Frank Lloyd Wright, *An Autobiography*

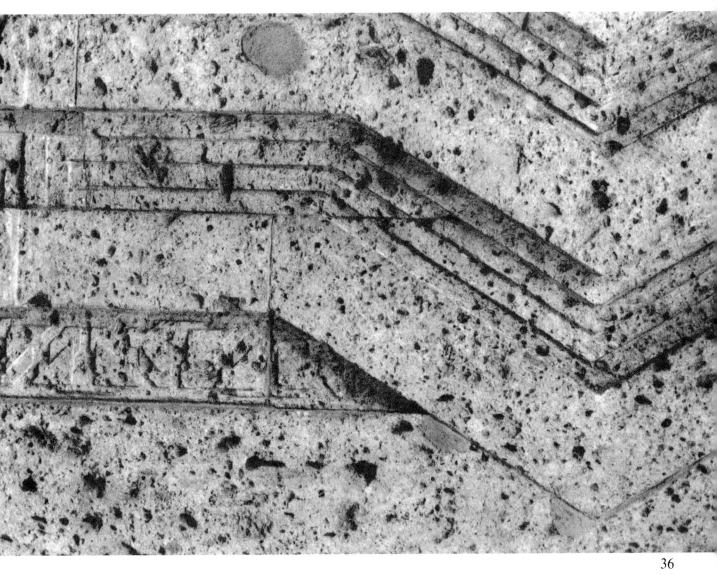

36

41

51

Five lines where three are enough is always stupidity. Nine pounds where three are sufficient is obesity. But to eliminate expressive words in speaking or writing—words that intensify or vivify meaning is not simplicity. Nor is similar elimination in architecture simplicity. It may be and usually is, stupidity.

In architecture, expressive changes of surface, emphasis of line especially textures of materials or imaginative pattern may go to make facts more eloquent—form more significant. Elimination, therefore, may be just as meaningless as elaboration, perhaps more often so.

—FRANK LLOYD WRIGHT, *An Autobiography*

53

58

What is architecture anyway? Is it the vast collection of the various buildings which have been built to please the varying taste of the various lords of mankind? I think not. No, I know that architecture is life; or at least it is life itself taking *form* and therefore it is the truest record of life as it was lived in the world yesterday, as it is lived today or ever will be lived. So architecture I know to be a Great Spirit. It can never be something which consists of the buildings which have been built by man on earth . . . mostly now a rubbish heap or soon to be one. Architecture is that great living creative spirit which from generation to generation, from age to age, proceeds, persists, creates, according to the nature of man, and his circumstances as they change. That is really architecture.

—FRANK LLOYD WRIGHT, *Frank Lloyd Wright on Architecture*

CAPTIONS TO PLATES

PLATE 1
Stone urn at porte-cochere.

PLATE 2
Fireplace front in parlor.

PLATE 3
Statue and pool at entrance court.

PLATE 4
Exterior door, guest wing.

PLATE 5
Detail of north guest-wing wall.

PLATE 6
Windows beside main entrance.

PLATE 7
Detail of exterior corner, side lounge.

PLATE 8
Guest wing at entrance court.

PLATE 9
North side of north guest wing.

PLATE 10
Pool and main entrance.

PLATE 11
View through side lounge windows to guest wing.

PLATE 12
Main lobby from third level.

PLATE 13
Main lobby from second level.

PLATE 14
Detail of main lobby.

PLATE 15
Corner of main lobby.

PLATE 16
Corner of side lounge.

PLATE 17
Steps to side lounge.

PLATE 18
View up to side lounge.

PLATE 19
Guest wing from dining room

PLATE 20
Corridor beside dining
room and view into
interior garden.

PLATE 21
Interior garden and terrace.

PLATE 22
Detail of guest wing.

PLATE 23
Detail of stone mullion,
mezzanine of main lobby.

PLATE 24
Detail of exterior corner,
side lounge.

PLATE 25
Detail of stone decoration.

PLATE 26
Base of wall at side lounge.

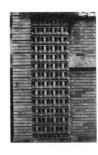

PLATE 27
Detail of terra cotta grille.

PLATE 28
Detail of pierced brick grille and
stone band.

PLATE 29
Detail of interior of guest wing.

PLATE 30
Detail of guest-room door.

PLATE 31
Exposed plumbing, guest wash basin.

PLATE 37
Detail of molded brick at base.

PLATE 32
Exposed plumbing, guest bathroom.

PLATE 38
Detail of stone ornament in dining room.

PLATE 33
Detail of carpet pattern at theater.

PLATE 39
Main dining room.

PLATE 34
Detail of stone on fireplace front in parlor.

PLATE 40
Columns, main dining room.

PLATE 35
Fireplace front in parlor.

PLATE 41
Theater seating 500.

PLATE 36
Detail of stone decoration.

PLATE 42
Special box in theater.

PLATE 48
Exterior corner of Peacock Room.

PLATE 43
View of long promenade.

PLATE 44
Column capital and gallery at promenade.

PLATE 49
Fireplace at side lounge.

PLATE 45
East end of guest-room wing with bridge to new building.

PLATE 50
Light at stairs, guest wing.

PLATE 46
East end of north guest wing.

PLATE 51
Detail of guest-room window.

PLATE 47
Detail of balcony, guest wing.

PLATE 52
Guest-wing wall.

PLATE 53
Windows of third level,
guest wing.

PLATE 58
Entrance and porte-cochere.

PLATE 54
Detail of elevator tower,
guest wing.

PLATE 59
Bust of Baron Okura, interior
garden.

PLATE 55
Partial view of main
entrance.

PLATE 60
Decorated column at
promenade entrance.

PLATE 56
Detail of exterior corner,
side lounge.

PLATE 61
Detail of stone brackets at
dining room.

PLATE 62
Exterior of side lounge.

PLATE 57
Detail of stone urn,
interior garden.

PLATE 63
Stone urn at north guest wing.

BIBLIOGRAPHY

Wright, Frank Lloyd: *An Autobiography*, 2nd ed., New York, 1943
————: *Frank Lloyd Wright on Architecture, Selected Writings 1894–1940*, edited by Frederick Gutheim, New York, 1941

OTHER BOOKS BY FRANK LLOYD WRIGHT (chronological order)

Wright, Frank Lloyd: *Ausgeführte Bauten und Entwürfe*, Berlin, 1910, reprinted by Dover Publications, Inc., as *Drawings and Plans of Frank Lloyd Wright: The Early Period (1893–1909)*, 24457-1, New York, 1983
————: *The Japanese Print: An Interpretation*, Chicago, 1912, reprinted, New York, 1967
————: *Frank Lloyd Wright: The Lifework of an American Architect*, edited by Wendingsen, Santpoort, 1925, reprinted New York, 1965
————: *Modern Architecture: The Kahn Lectures for 1930*, Princeton, 1931
————: *When Democracy Builds*, New York, 1945, expanded as *The Living City*, New York, 1958
————: *Genius and the Mobocracy*, New York, 1949
————: *The Future of Architecture*, New York, 1953
————: *The Natural House*, New York, 1954
————: *An American Architecture*, edited by Edgar Kaufmann, New York, 1955
————: *A Testament*, New York, 1957
————: *Drawings for a Living Architecture*, New York, 1959
————: *Frank Lloyd Wright: Writings and Buildings*, selected by Kaufmann and Raeburn, New York, 1960

BOOKS ABOUT FRANK LLOYD WRIGHT

Drexler, Arthur: *The Drawings of Frank Lloyd Wright*, New York, 1962
Hitchcock, Henry-Russell: *In the Nature of Materials: The Buildings of Frank Lloyd Wright, 1887–1941*, New York, 1942

FLOOR PLANS

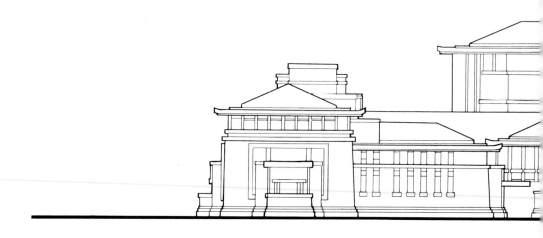

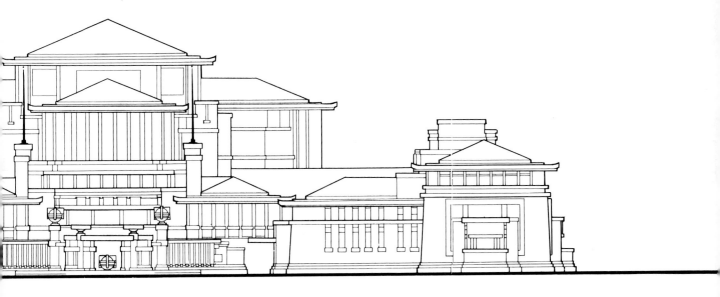

Figure 1. MAIN ELEVATION.

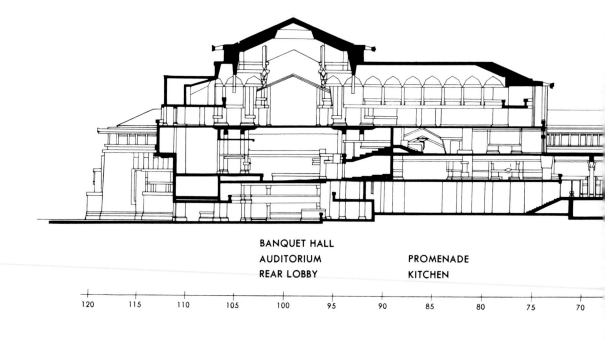

BANQUET HALL
AUDITORIUM   PROMENADE
REAR LOBBY   KITCHEN

120   115   110   105   100   95   90   85   80   75   70

Figure 2.

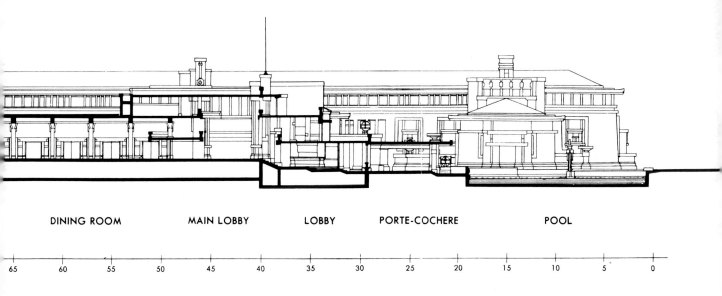

DINING ROOM   MAIN LOBBY   LOBBY   PORTE-COCHERE   POOL

65   60   55   50   45   40   35   30   25   20   15   10   5   0

ECTION AT CENTER LINE.

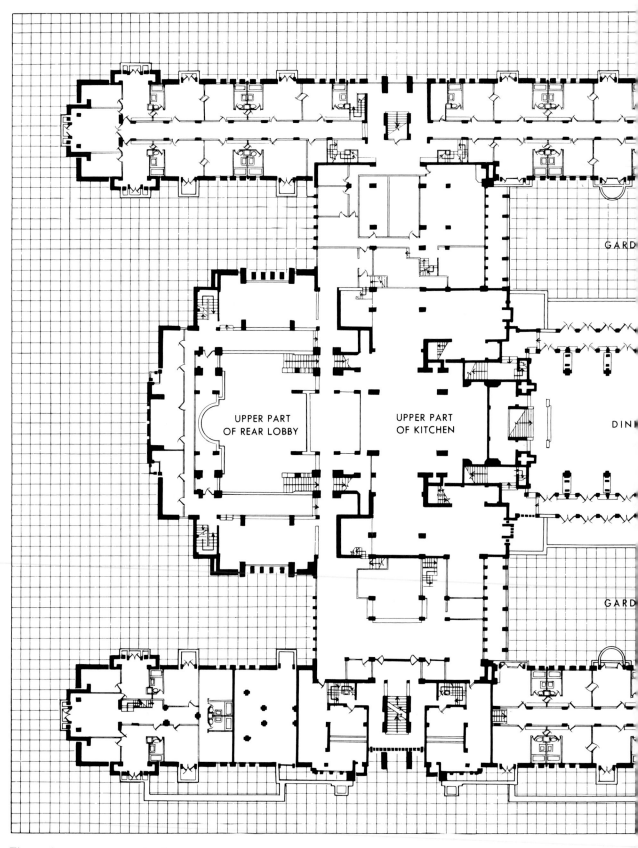

UPPER PART
OF REAR LOBBY

UPPER PART
OF KITCHEN

GARD

DIN

GARD

Figure 3. GROUND LEVEL.

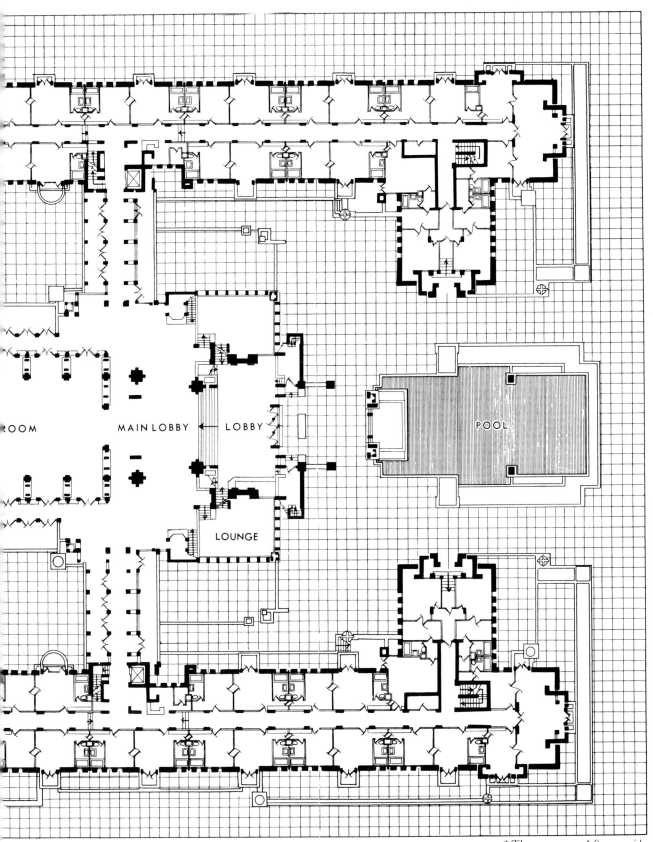

ROOM   MAIN LOBBY ← LOBBY   POOL

LOUNGE

*The squares are 4 ft. on a side.

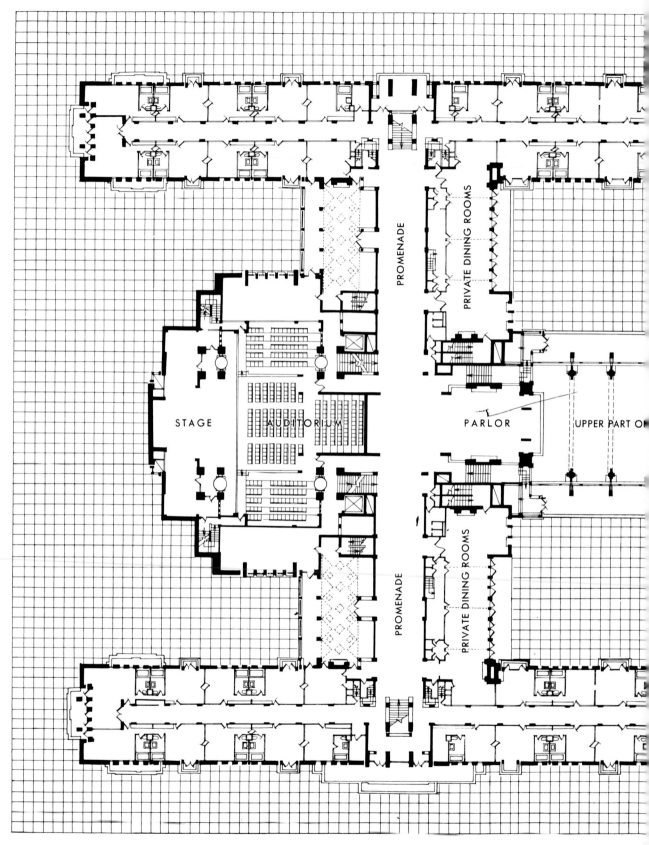

Figure 4. SECOND LEVEL.

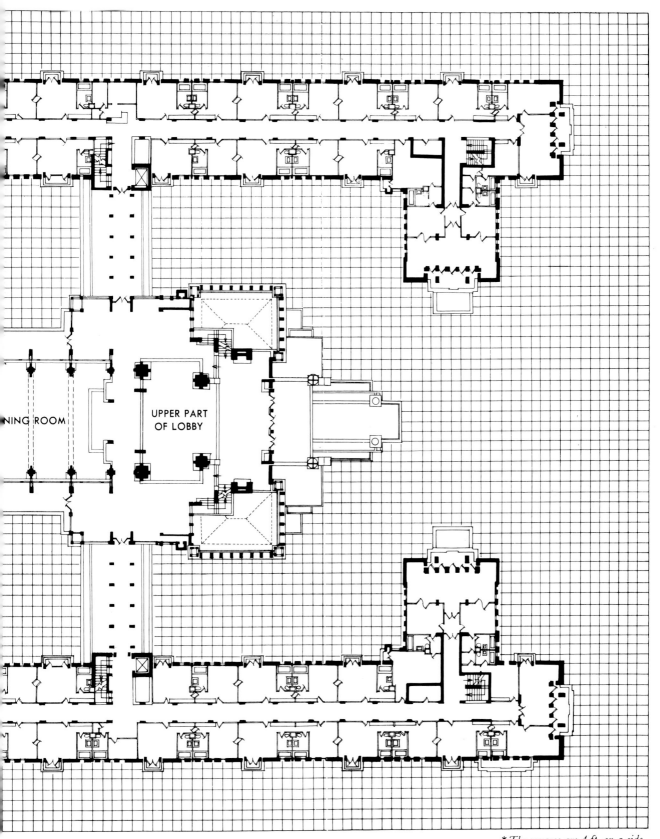

NING ROOM

UPPER PART
OF LOBBY

The squares are 4 ft. on a side.

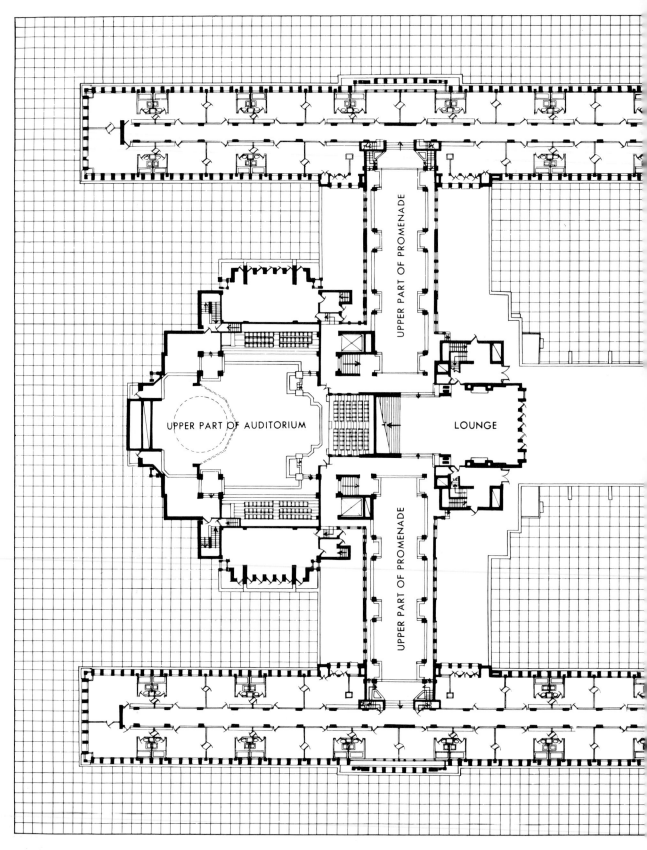

Figure 5. THIRD LEVEL.

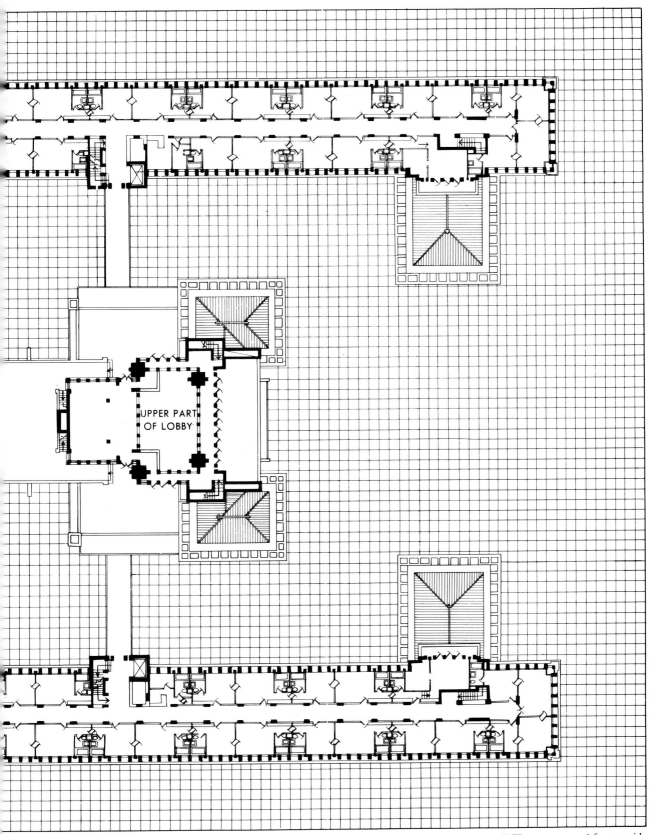

UPPER PART
OF LOBBY

*The squares are 4 ft. on a side.

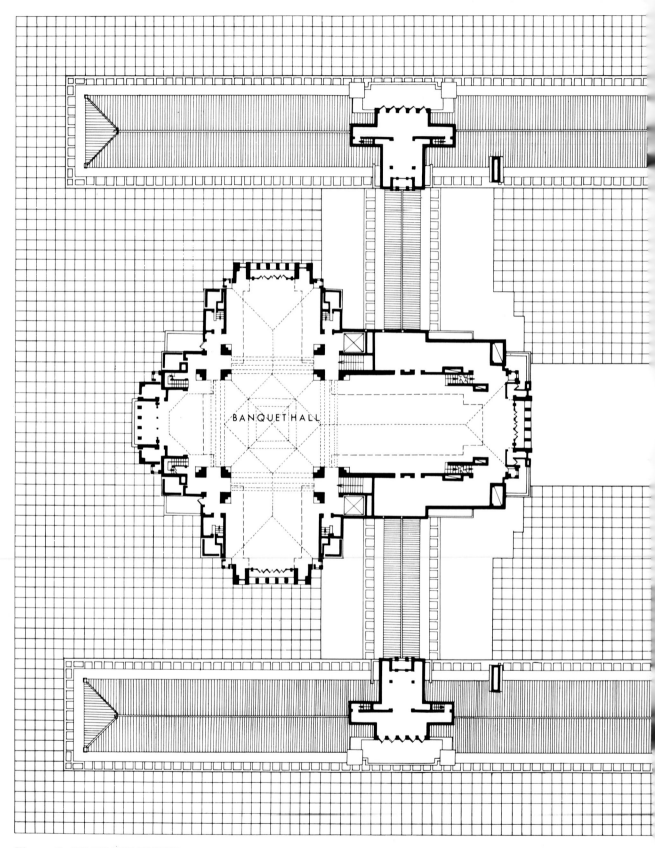

Figure 6. FOURTH LEVEL.

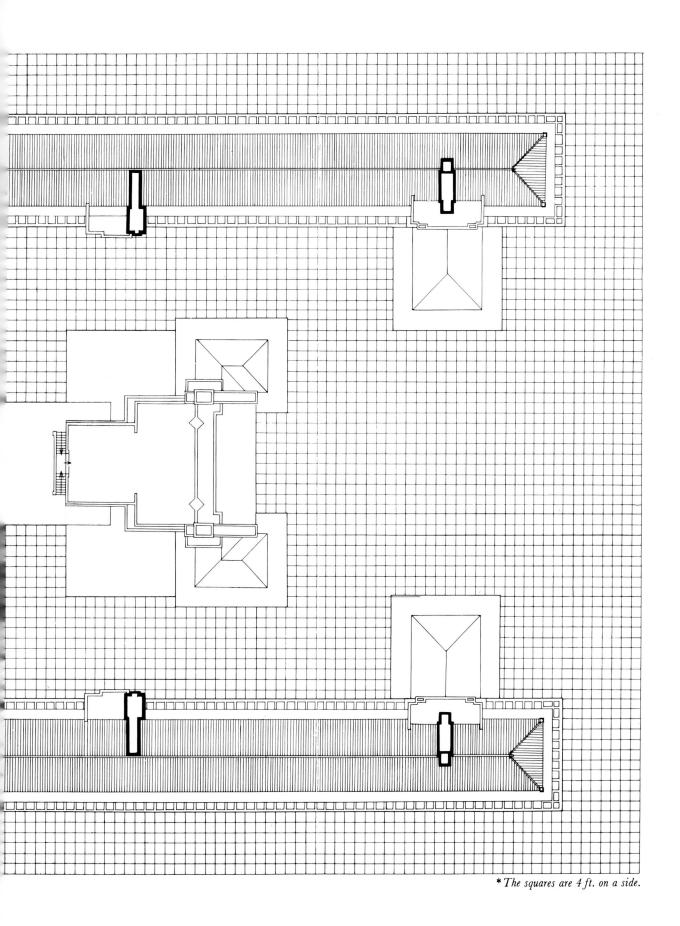

*The squares are 4 ft. on a side.